THE VOICE OF SHEILA CHANDRA

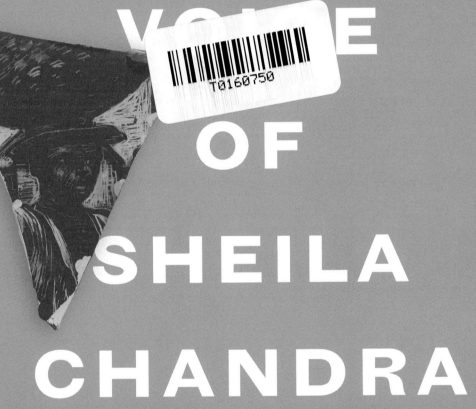

KAZIM ALI

10 9 8 7 6 5 4 3 2 1

Alice James Books are published by Alice James Poetry Cooperative, Inc.,
an affiliate of the University of Maine at Farmington.

Alice James Books
114 Prescott Street
Farmington, ME 04938
www.alicejamesbooks.org

Library of Congress Cataloging-in-Publication Data

Names: Ali, Kazim, 1971– author.
Title: The voice of Sheila Chandra / Kazim Ali.
Description: Farmington, ME : Alice James Books, 2020
Identifiers: LCCN 2020016123 (print) | LCCN 2020016124 (ebook)
    ISBN 9781948579124 (trade paperback) | ISBN 9781948579681 (epub)
Subjects: LCGFT: Poetry.
Classification: LCC PS3601.L375 V65 2020 (print) | LCC PS3601.L375 (ebook)
    DDC 811/.6—dc23
LC record available at https://lccn.loc.gov/2020016123
LC ebook record available at https://lccn.loc.gov/2020016124

Alice James Books gratefully acknowledges support from individual
donors, private foundations, the University of Maine at Farmington, the
National Endowment for the Arts, and the Amazon Literary Partnership.

Cover image: D'Ascenzo Studios, *Cotton Field* (broken), Philadelphia, 1932.
Vitreous enamel on plate glass, 12 x 9 ¼ in. (30.5 × 23.5 cm). Yale University
Photo: Yale University Art Gallery

THE VOICE OF SHEILA CHANDRA

ALICE JAMES BOOKS
Farmington, Maine
alicejamesbooks.org

TO OLGA BROUMAS AND T BEGLEY

Recite

Small animal recite
You sent nowhere
Arriving in the night
All my forgotten prayers
Not prayers really
Nothing to ask for
No one would answer
Crassness of calling
A body a corpse
Lawn mower sound
Through the window
The housekeeper singing
Is this body a house
Is this house a body
God's like you a misfit
You don't fit he don't fit

Hesperine for David Berger

Begin with the dining room attendant at the ivy-covered university who smashed the stained-glass window because we are now actually going to change history

Imagine then in the suburbs of Cleveland a sculpture of steel rings broken in halves but opening up away from the bullet-written history of the burning helicopter toward the open sky

Seems possible because there is a bridge between general relativity and quantum mechanics that no physicist has yet ascertained

Imagine neither a conditional future if the past were different nor forging ahead from the broken but something newer that bridged that loss

For example what if a painter left the canvas entirely and instead looked at all the extant surfaces in the already man-made and man-frayed world

History then as fragile as stained glass and yet writing new narratives that shape every movement forward

Both ways of understanding the behavior of matter cannot be true yet somehow they still behave as true on the lived-in planet

David Berger at 27 deciding to move across the world to Israel to train and compete in the Olympics 1972 Munich

What Corey Menafee did is he climbed up on top of a table in the dining room and with the long handle of his broom he

Sang in bits and pieces to god the road you knew which was the confusion road the one made of all your wrong turns

Geometry of a building makes it stand math is mighty there are abstractions in every letter their architecture makes sound possible

For each of you a practice Quran 5:48 says *if God had willed He would have just made you one people*

Imran Qureshi does not paint on canvasses but paints little blossoms on the ground on the wall in corners of the room they bloom like water or blood or light

While the Qawwali singer Amjad Sabri groans his throat open in ecstatic sound aiming to reach from the muck of the earth all the way into heaven

From the summit I plummet then into the time of unstrung lyres to try to go back into the dark time

A letter arriving in the night-mysterious reads *A reminder we do not forget we do not forgive*

Translator of frozen scripts you try to tongue your way through that old score shame that I am still trying to settle

Sky boat bear me down along these reticent cords while I plumb lupine fields in search of lingering snow

Do you know what your body is do you know what god is

Music that do sound off strings into voice from the body's drum that sings breathe through as wind

Shattered the panes of the stained-glass window depicting enslaved workers bearing cotton along a road

Hesperus the evening star shines with a cold light through the tightest drawn evenings sharp-edged and dissolute

He came into work in the dining room everyday and he hated that one image in the glass and one day he just

And of all that was wrong was a pattern painted not last year or a hundred years ago but I mean yesterday or this morning

Sun is going down on the wrong horizon, the sea glows green then blue then green again this is where I was born this in-between place

And so I curse the fucking dawn that grinds men to powder tears them from their bodies flings them down the hot dark barrel of a gun

How then to catalog the metadata of all the corpses that locate for us our own bodies and register their Western comfort

Bullet punching through a body like punching through a ticket registering it for passage

Do you know what god is what's not do you know what art is what's not do you know what a nation is a citizen a crime

Sir this world has always asked me for my labor then been silent upon delivery

Star of evening's twin brother was Phosphorus star of morning who rose up in the dawn and brought new day metaphor of course for new life

Savage spill and splendid this tended plot a plant this polity close to alarm smoke in the hallway the door opening the key stolen shadows appearing

What is the sound of misdemeanors hefting the minutes like prison tattoos when they took David Berger and his roommates and then five others in the second apartment sought

I crunch down in the room of my life to draw small blossoms in the corners of the world flowers or water or light what do I have against the intention of violence but these small chromatic gestures nothing

While I pretend the sound I howl has some direction this impossible world always a gate opening could be the death of me

What passes from beyond the horizon of the black hole can define how the universe is made because if we are right we are right but

The window shattered and glass rained down onto the street outside the worker was arrested but the university declined to press the charges

The beautiful were made beautiful the blood in their bodies sang and in the rain of white phosphorus into the streets of Gaza

This technique of Qawwali depends on the old belief that God is found in abstraction and in sound say the Sufi teachers it is the physical matter of the universe made

Theoretical physicist Stephon Alexander then plays a Coltrane riff and reveals its score which maps a shape that corresponds to the equation describing a particle of space-time

You did learn in painting directly on stone or the concrete sidewalk or the notes nesting in the throat or body against body wrestling or tumbling in space

Register then my ticket on the train in France the machine says *composter* and in that space between languages I am found

I have come back to this village on the Mediterranean shore after sixteen years who was I then the same age as David Berger same age as Mohammed Al-Khatib

Compost as in compost the old tomatoes into the earth make a complete system of the body's history into the future life

Are we then only particles of light and liquid and petaled material swirling one into the other lighthouse dark unlit instrument silent

But then the Greeks learned from the Babylonians that the evening star and the morning star that they had envisioned and made gods of and written poems about were in fact the same heavenly body

I register the old tomatoes back into the earth try to clear the trail of ants on the counter swarming the counter where I sliced them

We live by laws of men drawn of laws of gods men say are real who then erected the frame for this chainsaw night

And at this moment on the sea I see in the water a reflection of every face I've known each wave contains another wave each moment of violence contains

Architecture of the Holocaust Remembrance Center outside Jerusalem based on the Hebrew letter *yud* for memory or remembrance but does it remember the forests around it were the site of the destroyed village Deir Yassin

In either case we are inventing the past which means it changes the future which means the machine of time is real made of gears and parts

Register each body like tickets for the train

Munich 1972 the road leads right through young men's brightest hours no question of a Palestinian team not then not now

Ramallah 2016 Mohammed Al-Khatib laces up his running shoes ridiculously trying to train as a sprinter with neither spikes nor coach nor starting block

Each moment of time is a part of space and each piece of space-time is a physical object an object that can be graphed and mapped

Impossible to see impossible to feel to refract how finished the pattern that is every unfolding

Bright glass of many colors the slaves hauling cotton shattered and flickering down toward the concrete

What am I without these things but no question at all

And yet here is Coltrane mapping the nature of the universe in sound here is David Berger using his body to show the potential of strength Mohammed decides by guts and grit he can imagine himself faster

And so I shout down with ragged throat this encroaching blue that brings dawn then brightening day then David and his teammates hustled by the kidnappers into a helicopter bound for the airport promised passage out of Germany

There is no fajr call here on the seaside to alert me to the hour but I can hear creatures stirring from sleep a gift so like death it reeks

Night resounding with Coltrane's whining instrument his breath through brass has somehow arrived at the same calculation as

Mohammed seeks to shave tenths of seconds off his time there is no accounting for the decision of the body toward its sport

He would have made you one people but He wanted to try you, so strive alongside one another toward good deeds, to God you will all return and then he will account and explain to you the differences you had

Somehow sound improvised in time creates that geometric pattern of branches swirling or the equation that tells

At the beginning of the universe Amjad Sabri sings away for all he's worth his voice unspooling *soie sauvage* like a bolt of raw silk like an untamed spirit

He hopes to find God echolocate Him deep in the harmonic overtone perhaps at precisely the place his voice breaks

In the end it don't matter whether blood is particles or rivulets they spill just the same like Qureshi's painting of little red flowers rosettes of blood on the floor where the mass shooting took place his flowers covering the place where blood once marked

Or on walls following blue streams following the sewer pipe or the slicks of sunlight on the windowpane

This unending pattern of abstraction to say we can inscribe ourselves into the landscape we can change the past we can write ourselves as a letter arriving unannounced to god with no return address

What other explanation does any scholar have for the verses of the Quran that are neither sentences nor sayings but mere glyphs of letters

Alif Lam Mim

Ta Ha

Alif Lam Ra

And physics knows what Sabri is hungry for that the point of breaking a
bullet enters David Berger's left shoulder

Unlike the others he is shot while still in the apartment perhaps to intimidate
the other prisoners or perhaps he tried to resist

Because he saw the lip of the black hole as the possibility to know and it is
that which tipped us off that the systems do match

Everything thought was true still behaves as if it is true but both things
cannot in the lived-in universe be actually true

If we are on a continuum a wave where time and space bend then nothing is
supposed to emerge from the event horizon and yet

Corey Menafee climbed up on the table he just said *It's 2016 I shouldn't have
to come to work and see things like that That thing's coming down today I'm tired of it*

Mohammed left Palestine to go to Houston Texas where he found enough
open space to run and train *I only wanted to hear Palestine's anthem in the stadium*
he said

To hear is to make real

Coltrane was a physicist

Sabri found a way to God

David Berger left his home in Cleveland to move to Israel to lift weights and compete and so at the end of it when the bodies of the ten others return to Israel David's body is flown back to the States alone

These boys' bodies are made of particles that travel one into the other and I curse the crepuscular moment dark and light what are you what is god what isn't

Not until epochs of time later did the Romans look into the sky at Phosphorus whose name means Bearer of Light and translate into their own language as Lucifer

Called also Son of Morning

Does every journey continue down the barrel of a gun from the Olympic village to the helicopter to the airport where the trick was played to the shootout to the firestorm

What sound breaks the circle of action and reaction

If space do bend then time

Can history be unwoven the tightness released to make it possible to breathe and write anew

Are we pieces made up of pieces made up of pieces

In little licks like a mother cleaning a baby with her animal tongue Sabri draws red petals into the air in sound

David Berger's body straining to life or Mohammed's body racing

Grey endless stone in the cemetery in the suburb of Cleveland I wandered looking for the grave

Sound emerges the sound of the sea from the blue saxophone notes trickling from Qureshi's paintbrush

Glass littering down the window to the street clear the sun shines through

In the suburbs of Cleveland past the shopping mall through the office park nestled up against the interstate is a pedestal of black steel broken rings

Do you even know at all or do you just have to sing to find the place a voice breaks

There is no tradition in the literature of the world of the hesperine not a serenade nor an aubade but rather a curse to first darkness itself begging it not to fall a poem against the falling of night to ward off death the first mortal death was murder and so all this geometry may be inevitable a tired rehearsal

The stones I left on David's tomb mark what in the end may be just my passing that a living person was very briefly here looking to touch the dead

So do we have to just reach up and shatter it that image of David and his teammates held at gunpoint in the apartment the police so anxious to move them from the Olympic Village

Broken circles that approach the sky the way a flower would or a fountain or a bird

Can we sing over the noise or paint down on the stone once marked by flesh and death can we move forward without breaking

As Sabri's voice breaks his body breaks he wonders does it always happen that the divine begins when the mortal is shattered

A gunshot begins the race

Dusk turns then to night turns to dawn then turns to day bodies infect and inflect each other with particles small moments of light and dark

Qureshi paints another little red flower down do he pray that history may be erased by beauty

How can one create in painting in sound in the poetry of the body the new and abiding future life

Bodies separated by years and miles and religion and law may release their own energy may transfer into one another may be the same body

Is the reality of the physical universe a continuum of time and space or is it made of moments that can move backward and forward can the past be changed

Hesperus makes a play for the sacred space of grief Phosporus rains down upon Gaza into the bodies of unmade sprinters weight lifters pole vaulters gymnasts

What if God is improvising like Coltrane

Ta Sin Mim

There's no time left David has a plane to catch says good-bye to his parents

'Ain Sin Qaf

The broomstick shatters the glass window and the image litters down

Kaf Ha Ya 'Ain Suad

A voice then breaks as evening covers us in a downpour what else what else

Ya Sin

End then not in the present moment nor in some deathless wished for past but somewhere very ordinary a normal day a spring day perhaps a little chilly there is Mohammed in the hills above Ramallah lacing up even though there is no open ground to run no coach to train him no spikes for his shoes no starting blocks

Know No Name

Know no name
Why this holy day honed
Hollow day haul
I lost wind when wooden
I can't bear to be
Unaided in hunt unhanded
To haunt when strewn sound
Who will be held in hand
Brought sent
Mooring at the shore
Who're you for
For what fewer who wore
Be called this wooer
More who are the ones
In horror to light will strew
then sue for war

The Voice of Sheila Chandra

Breaks is constant was like
The river light on the river
Riven that remained a rift
An old rill that sounded
She merged with the vibe
Ration of the drum a hum a
Home womb and um
She OM moaned in the loam
Dark earth come Sheila
Dame ocean dome this poem
Roam to tome tomb foam
Original fountain that fed
My mom Zam-zam when I
Was born

Who can in syllables like
Sheila Chandra moan us
Covered in a blanket of sound
This like cloud bank of stars
Keeping us from eternity
Which under the blanket seen
Like Sanjay a dancer who I
Somehow look like was mistook
For three times in one day
Twenty years ago but the story
Still resounds some woman
At a festival saw him perform
Swore I was he I said I wasn't she
Did not believe

Me brass bowl soul swindle
Through years no identity theft
I want to move like that off the axis
Of the spine into where and where
Sanjay said I am not him and what
Does all this have to do with the voice
Of Sheila Chandra she having lost
Having now no longer sound
Now a constant striking into chaos
That note that flickers through
In abstraction one is one or zero
And confused the ear does not
Focus neither opens nor closes
Always is

Long before she lost it drift–
S unanchored wanted to merge
And the body of the singer become
The body of the instrument
Talk to the drum find it hum
Study its vowels she made her vow
To sound slowly syllable by
Syllable she pronounced words
In Uzbek word unmoored word
Pure sound oh river long had I
Been long seasons invaded
By your current devoured your tongue
Of water those years time bent
My one voice spoke

Carried cacophony world wheel
Into the human one small voice
Box pool swum midnight we went
Into the sea expecting our prayers
Might carry themselves across
The silver-slammed surface would
Be answered or do they answer
Pale cut of prayers do not answer
Like back into the dark water what
Are those stripes of light across
The room a shape that evaporates
Upon waking what language cannot
Hold onto what you cannot
Hold onto

Closer the wire against my shins warns
Me from falling blue into the painting is
Always a web each cell holding a prisoner
Of thought wire is god where is what
Goes through a cute short thick bearded
Guy's mind with the tape measure and the keys
On his belt I've been following holds
The bathroom door open one second
Too long and I nearly follow him
Inside but body language is hard
To read I stayed with the painting and
Now he too is staring into *The Islands*
And writing Agnes Motha Fucka Martin
In his notebook

Smoke a voice hits all the notes at once
Devotional or pop song or drone same
Difference talk now body as stone I am
Walking backwards from death through
Porn and prayer why shouldn't I fuck
A stranger in the Guggenheim bathroom
While someone bangs on the door return
To unknowing where Sheila found
Me where who found me Dog Star my
Friend neither day nor night nor
Behind the wire but tell in the fragile body
What's next how did I get caught not
Listening when what happened the fortune-
Teller told

Now do I always turn to the tenor stricken
I have no fear of god but of being
This archangel unfolding to emerge
From god into form how untoward
Above and below the line of having lived
I abstain bound to the horizon not
Earth not sky not Sheila sings the voice
Breaks body breaks stations of the cross or
Jewish texts that blank out one vowel
Unspeakable Zen mind is not empty
Mind but mind river knows it flows let me
Get there past years or drink or sex when I
Saw the dog after a decade he only wanted to
Look at me lick me smell me

How to transcribe what flickers what is not
Fixed that voice letters made not of ink but light
Not words of fire on stone how do you transcribe
The blank vowel all the after that aerates
Not disappear but settle down through air
You do not want to say but sing where might
Be rain be sky come down by snow but know
You invite it to cover you the blanket your coat
A heavy pressure god pressure of rain you want
To start the song over but do not dare to be ready
No tune no cadence nothing to pick up no bridge
To cross now to be small again break through
there is no beginning to any song only the place
the singer picks up the tune

At the café on a Sunday morning you
Spot your friend across the room
Who is maybe in a hurry and pretends
Not to see you and you've forgotten
Your glasses so you can pretend you
Did not notice her trying to pretend she
Did not see you outside there is a river
And everyone is waiting how boring god
Is everywhere how boring we are all
Water she'd rather face the rain than
Say hello or continue the line of the painful
Fiction impossible to see this voice im-
Possible to map such failure how finished
Nothing night day that I drain

What represses unhomes in the sound
Who has made me what is made me
Is a voice just muscles and shape and
Breath to phrase a song boats assemble
At the mouth of the harbor mouth in
Earth you who wrote an ode to silence
Never wrote of what is silenced I did
Seek all resounding caves let the voice
Be lit all the lanterns in the new world we
Need the language of stone from string
To string quiver in the opening the garden
So beautiful Lucifer dark sun of morning
No Eden but innocence no expulsion
But after

Dark painting I saw once at SFMOMA so dark
I could not see it so dark I did not know if it was
Protruding from the wall or recessed into it
Quiver I did quake because dizzy I was
Unknowable surface god August 2 the town
Is different I am not in flames small boats
Steer across the harbor the Cap Canaille
Governs every view sixteen years since I
Came I remember a wide open plaza a stone
Staircase down to the sea blue now and the town
Thick with restless voyagers I die into what
Comes open all the windows tie back the
Curtains I hope the furious mistral finds its
Way in I am late for dinner

In New York once I took a friend to a party
He kissed every man in the room including
The waitstaff the bartender and the program
Director of the foundation I don't know where
To say my home is anymore when someone
Asks I say I live out of a suitcase but not well
Sun sparkling on the water town signs warn
Of wildfires cicadas and boat engines long hallway
From my room to the stairs lined with discarded
Pieces of furniture dressers chairs end table
I open my window to the sea the storm a roar
Is a kind of silence at dinner someone says I am
Staying in Virginia Woolf's room that the furniture
Was painted by Vanessa Bell

August 3 last night I was so lonely it felt
Like death to sleep to be seen from
A precipice yet I delve down do not climb
To places in the world I am called to how
One turns one's back on a calling in the
Afternoon Eleanna's fearlessly bad French
I don't know much about music and never
Knew enough words to explain myself
About anything in Latin Hindi and open
Sounds Sheila tells moon or night or sea oh
Or Uzbek don't look like I remember
The sun vetoes all my panaceas that sky
And water are the same object now choose
There said it better now

Music spent my breath to achieve or invent
Death each chord or cadence out of
Reach out of tune last time in this town
I promised vow or vowel to turn
My back forever on chaos and give
Myself instead to music organizing
Itself in my ear from chaos a river
Made rather than music that makes
A shape of endless seconds I devoted
Myself to the equation of numbers
Between each sound a formula that
Matches planets and atoms music
Is not an art but science I could have
Remained alive but I broke

No more will I listen to other than
A single note moaned not known
I do not here think again what place
Presents here a body as a battery
Of the one moment to open
Your mouth to plug in I will allow what
I invented to find its color make
A shape which neither water nor
Sky do how do you now in this
Contained shape go through
Your life not like a constellation
Not guessed at intuited or divined
No name so how do you discern a shape for
What is often called god

Ocean is a dress a woman might wear like I
Would wear with dark lips and smoky eyes
like the vow I abandoned in the hills last time
I signed up for math and anger I return
emerging and from the ocean of electronic
sound letters come recounting every
past day I know god comes only in
madness and mess then a photo of Carolyn
and I on the shore of the cold cold lake
exchanging secrets of translation and lust
sitting down on the bench I take refuge
in the lord of thyme lord of the storm
Lord oh lord this lake Carolyn gone
Water too cold to swim in

I opened all the windows to let the storm in
Everything in the room scatters or
Is it shatters yesterday I climbed up
The Cap Canaille I felt no feeling
Of worship of the body's ability no bliss
No work nothing at the end
of it Christianity is a trick
of power the letter flies from
my hand before I am ready it is
Sent before I know it already failed
in the wake of Carolyn's death
Her husband packed up her mother's crystal
to sell he said under his breath all
These things no one wants

Sheila Chandra sings without words
Because a word is a form of rage at
Death the implicit formlessness
Of the body which translates as
The soul does not cohere every
Feeling of a body as mortal means
Separately French *mot* and *mort*
What do we know and can't tell
Of the deep black of the world of
Death of the painting on the wall
I in past days trusted border
Zones relinquished homes sounds
Let the nothing storm in
Was it a sculpture or a recess

These stone staircases lead
Nowhere or everywhere but
Not to any house church or
Bar I can find they never lead
Anywhere I choose my way
Back to the village in full sun
Meaning no stars to guide me
Nor instinct to creep I still do
Not know how to sing bright
Cool light no avenue no water
No trustworthy direction only
Whose shape I fathom whose
Edges I only discern by touch
Smell or taste

Vantablack was made for missiles
Or planes for defense purposes so dark
No eye could see it some voices are
Like that no one could hear them it
Is not good to be lost to be lost is
More than metaphor for spiritual
Condition I sit at the terrace overlooking
The green sea perhaps it is failure
That ought to be sought the voice
That fails falls silent Sheila's or
The body's the blue failed me the sun
Fails every evening I we you have all
Failed too everyone who strove all these
Long years for peace failed

August 7 predawn blue and blue the sound
On the water fishing boats closer than I
Imagined no one is awake some animals
Maybe what I do without knowing in a
Harrowing world what I do without knowing
As I listen to the gurgle of water against
The promontory I feel like I am listening
To a body how slow and opening a piece
Of tune where one does not know how
It will unfold no chord or cadence to tell
You in sound what the path will be how
It will happen until it happens I do not want
To be alone what does it mean anyway when
Someone says Muslim

Yesterday as we started hiking my stomach
Turned so quickly I had to run
Into the bushes and hardly had enough time
To pull down my pants and squat before I
Shat myself empty then when we returned
Home and showered Philippe came and he adored
My body all afternoon licked my skin he buried
His face in my armpits and breathed in deeply
Held my feet to his lips caressed and kissed them and
After we lay sweaty and talked about Duras about
This hotel by the sea how it is like the places
In her novels I said let me smell and lick your
Body too because to shit and to fuck are
Two main purposes of art

When the sun goes down you move
Horizontal you become everything
In the world at once rather than waking
Like vertical where you obsess over
Ascend or descend or whatever rain
At the edge of the building spit forth
By gargoyles does drown yourself in the jizz
Of the world no shape of narrative
I'm lost but thrilled sun yellow still
Inside my self I am a pocket for the other
Day already gone Sheila hillbilly
Iconoclast seizes the song in the cage
Of her throat drawls not the edge of it
But its music entire

Sheila Chandra has been rendered mute
The ambassador of sound gray clouds
Compromise the day auctioned off
Siphoned off betrayed by the failure
Of nerve endings and science no cure
For Burning Mouth Syndrome she sang
In Uzbek contorted her tongue around
Words she never knew learned even
The language of the drum away from
Melody there is only harmony in the
Outer districts of the city of sound ordinary
Spaces empty bandstand atonal landscape
Sea's surface in the morning before the day
Traffics its contours

In a world governed by storm and noise why
Then should a singer not fall silent though
By great suffering her mouth that orchestra
Hall aflame the drone her most miniscule
Movement still do the echoes resound
Even now can I discern them Anish Kapoor
Explores the place sight disappears rich
Dark that opens he makes shapes of them
Invites you to understand or learn where
The effort to understand fails Agnes
Martin her shapes of white absence both
What when the throat fails sounds out does
Sheila still listen to music what does it
Sound like

Can she still feel music in her body can she
Vocalize even without technology of the
Mouth tongue palate glottis vocal cords
What is a voice Anish Kapoor granted
Exclusive right to work with Vanta-
Black she now communicates through notes
And gesture Vantablack made for
Military purposes like sound also used
For torture all sounds to wake you vibrate
Your brain what emerges as an echo from
Music as torture children on the beach
Playing god is sound or art or science
Shit and sex the body's echo what mess
Is left in the big or the little death

Matisse did not believe but wanted to
On the walls the podium the priests'
Chasubles upstairs in the chapel draw
His faith in art for him everything even
Clothing was a part of architecture inspired by
The nun's original drawing he undertook
The commission but did not use her plan
Named Marie after *mare* the bitterness
Of the sea I tremble with Eleanna
In the cold boat we are far
From the shore and the sun is spent we are
Buoys that bob but are monstrous beneath
The surface all music deafening or a form
of shouting when you are lost

Is the voice to know or to know
The edge of knowing Muslims do not
Depict or particularize God only gesture
With blank spaces Ali Kazim does not
Paint with a brush but pounds powdered
Pigment right into the paper he compromises
Masculinity by picturing a muscular
Man with a flower tucked behind his
Ear shaving himself with a straight razor
He reinvents manhood as a form of
The feminine texture of a voice breaks in 2007
I saw a Catalan *Antigone* and at the moment
Of her incomprehensibility the actress began
Screaming in English

Calligraphy is a meeting point
Between abstract and particular
By certain combinations of visual
Marks to make symbols Chandra
Lost her voice around the same
Time I found mine at midnight
We went to swim in the sea so
We could be in the dark and not
Know the bottom but the moon
Lit up the surface so silver so
Slammed and then the boy
With the fear of failure falling
Architecture voice God depths death
He swam

Rain comes down I have not
Returned no voice to contour
My tongue nor ear no nobody
Not Ritsos not Wright
Not Lee Ali Valentine Howe
Not Revell Cooper Clifton
Not Darwish Dickinson not nobody
I pull myself together I imagine
Lines that spool and return rather
Than the rhythm of the sea a darker
Meter one that can't be discerned
Don't know the edge of I will not
Map my way back I will
Not look I will

One cannot manipulate expression or
Do you fold and fold your voice fool
Sound is sound the building block
Of the universe sea so clear I can see
Thirty feet down even from the terrace
The waves roar and the conversation
Of those out on the water somehow
Carries sound of ice melting in my
Glass of boat engines the singing
Insects everything interrupts I hid
In the Matisse Chapel I did not want
To know how the shape of sound
Appears an object grows more powerful
In the imagination

Sheila's voice always in the background
Always disappearing into the music
Of what surrounds it the way one loses
Onself in sex or death or the moment
Of shitting I got lost in Salman's
Music he said it was a surrender of
Ego when he left me behind but really
It was a surrender of my will words too
Have god inside but for the prize of
The body they do not compete can-
Not hold the storm of time cannot
Hold the line do I touch the ocean
Inside will my family come to
My funeral

That night we swam the full moon
Civilized us federated us gave us
Our nationality we who were lost
I have now lost what little heritage
I did have returned to the rude
Rough world long vowels of
Morning evening birds scream
No soft blanket falling to cover
But a throttling a suffocation
Of dusk no silence when the self
Stills the absence of noise is itself
Torture I cannot sleep tongued loose
Drones move through a riff by
A singer without papers

August 9 Eleanna takes me out on
The water Miller exploding the form
Of the novel itself I see now how Nin
Wanted to move away from his vociferous
Singing of the world as material to try
To construct a music of the way
The mind works still fed by light on the
Water a mute noise of engines under
Water as the boat passes the light-
House and heads out for open sea
Remembering in Palestine crawling
Down the hill trying to catch a wifi
Signal from the settlement untapped
Improvisation of space

At the stone terrace the gardener lingers
Clipping hedges while I work
One of the men targeted by Mossad
After the Olympics was a poet killed
In the street his poems untranslated
All the artists and writers killed the open
Space of the sea yesterday Eleanna and I
Went too far out went almost all the way
To Marseille we saw the pink-grey sky
Of wildfire I accepted the waves I found
In the chapters of the Quran to sing my
Way through turbulence draw a way
Through the waves savage wildfire and
The villages evacuated

We woke to the smell of burning air
A little cool smell of charred refuse
Colors muted last night the moon
Came clear nearly blue eyes too
Painfully large rough on the eyes and
Impatient but I wanted to look so
Badly for the meteors the sea
Crashing against the rocks smoke
From the fire obscured the sky
In the morning we rowed across
The harbor and realized fear of heights
And fear of depth is the same just one
You see and one
you don't

An hour or more of pulling oars
Boat pitching up and down I sing
Verses to save us what was it that
Soothed me god's words the rhythm
And rhyme my own voice the memory
Of my father's voice or my mother's
Voice all of these none of these the sea
Changes it is a friend we rowed around
The rocks our fingers getting bashed to
Stay on course you have to pay attention
At every minute the boat drifts rockward
Or seaward never in one direction I lay
On my back listening to a crackling is it in
the water or in me

Oh in the hows of Sheila Chandra
Sigh lents dew knot rain
She, la Chandh-Ra's voice that swells
Of sun I am won what word quells
The chords in the box the mouth
Throat third voice sought
Dew naut reign in rain my hands
Hand me the rein will you sing can
You swing your votes vox fox
In the *howza* I learned scripture
Stripped her in the roost roust
All the birds to the blue the Moon-Sun
Singer singes now the world sound
Some echo wind echo wing

Who can born then believe
Beleaguered besieged be seen
Leagues from where you started
Parted in league with my liege
Legions of sound sound sounder
Her then be leaved darkest black
And be unseen a voice tracks back
For frown fawn fawned founded
Fundament firmly this firmament
This fund of sound born when you are
I did not want to be found how
Can you say that how can you now
Know what foe no she sang out flow
She breathed be real eve and lo

Tagaq Sutra

Pilgrim in parts
Ply the route entire entre
mensonge and mon songe
Woke in second sleep
Caught in the rain
Eon a season
Sees one broke urn
Trees turn autumnal
Ought one turn to know
Where unfolds eyrie or kyrie
Sound none reason earn to tourn
Whole night now none torren

Phosphorus

Is it true then that Berlin is a city you write yourself against
Unlike New York or Paris which write themselves into you
That the city itself has no voice or
If it has one it agrees to mute
Itself against the noise of your own life

Or is it a chorus of voices sedimented
A voice in which the present life is overlaid
On voices from history
An aural palimpsest
Ghost town with golden stumbling blocks in the street

For example on this night seven years ago I went
To go to a party where ready to dance
We ended up not dancing but talking
About how far away
From our families we all were

Where I put my arm around my friends to try to keep them
In my life but didn't we scatter like people scatter
One of those friends died on a winter hike
Another moved to Berlin and the last I lost touch with
But heard from a friend he had gone to Moldova to teach English

Voices like on the old answering machine when the tape
Had been recorded on over and over again
Like those old messages left for each other
When you called a lover you would try to leave a very long message
To use up the whole tape so he knew your absent passion

It's a bad metaphor not because there are no tapes anymore but because
The lover in question is married now has a house a wife stepchildren
I called him once and left the message I never heard back did he hear it or did she
Am I Hesperus the Son of Evening who like Orpheus looks back at what's gone
Or Phosphorus light-bringer Son of Morning looking to uncover what's next

*

Bodies that walk through
The world represent spectacular confluences of historic possibilities
Playing out over millennia
The men I've loved all of them have been dark quiet deep passive
I was always the fire

Perhaps that is why I linger in cities of beauty
Want to myself lie down and be ravished even brutalized
Fair to say even on my good days I'm not the wisest decision-maker
Lost in the sunset at the Brandenburg Gate the brass band plays
Of all the music in the world to choose from American rock and roll

In crystal frequency the rock talks to the water
Inside your body sounds resound
Everyone asks me questions and I do not answer
I just say whatever I feel like and no one cross-examines me
I don't want to tell about how I only unleash my shame to wander when I—

Oh but that's one of the things I want to not tell
City not of my city
Forty days pass and what am I now
An account of old losses depends on the archive of flesh
A person is not made new but quivers in place

Never to make or exist exit evince evict
All old lovers and friends linger a river that winds
Along years long he corners what he can make
Follows the pattern of wind
Why were you really afraid

You believe you are wicked but it's the world
That changes position
No one will care for you
And yet you are held down or held up
Be not abandoned the wind has its own demands

Always you are afraid to say
You were not loved
You have no family
This is how you disappear
We learned on our own how to live how to speak

Trees my familiar ones fallen in the storm
Our house is in danger the storm touches down
And flies into the sky the stream the years we lived there
Flow through me and say will the boy ever be happy
Sound of crystal sound of a glass harmonica

The length of a life spun by the younger sister cut by the older
The forgotten middle child worries the thread in her hands
If we have to choose between mythologies I choose the one
With the father who had two sons but only one at a time
And God asked him to sacrifice the lonely son I want to be saved

So my father could learn to love me
So I could help save my other sister
But the myth goes badly wrong
I am not Isaac nor Ishmael nor any other son who was saved
In this story I am the ram

*

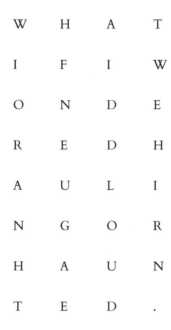

W   H   A   T

I   F   I   W

O   N   D   E

R   E   D   H

A   U   L   I

N   G   O   R

H   A   U   N

T   E   D   .

*

Translator of shadows invite the waking the world
Gray filmed by rain
Rain not even present but suffusing the experience
More unfamiliar in the world
A dream book is one in which you have to record

But I won't
Sound always lets you
But what if
Just what if
Sound was a metaphor for something past it

You're setting up vibrational patterns
An echo of language a song to trick the dead from the other side
Vibration is only one sound of it
An echo of the sound unmade
Unstruck

Your body itself an echo of unstruck sound
Evidence in the waking world of the dream
All of this unreal
Playing out in ripples
Something spoken unspoken

Poem unspoken
Leaves falling wind long-missed lover
I drink the crystal stone-infused water
I try to remember but there is nothing to remember
A room or a city seen through a window

Square it is a city with a real geography
Page a place you actually happen
In touch to world moves eros tenderness violence
Coaxed to movement
I take everything you say very seriously

*

T	O	H	A
V	E	T	H
E	C	O	U
R	A	G	E
T	O	D	I
G	S	O	D
E	E	P	.

*

Fire translates the forest to ash
Tree translates water from dirt into leaf
Leaf translates sun into green
Sun translates a body
Magnetic poles of the planet translate the

Dancer on the stage
Knows in cities language is found
A person crossing the street
Sunday morning in the garden
Lemon flowers dropping in the pool

I haven't yet made the worst of my mistakes
The river is my governor
The tree out the window legislates pure rules
Sun and wind guide me
Name of green guide me

And like a beast I bolted free
Left the father empty-handed
Unable to offer anything to God but
Isaac's terror or Ishmael's obedience
Both in vain

Will I be forgiven
For making a break for it
By either the father or God or the sons
One too obedient to complain
The other too frightened to move

We don't know where we're going
We must be brave enough
Attention is dangerous—it has brought you to this despair
Sometimes I think god is a dog
Slinking along breaking his agreements

All right radio tune into the blanket of sound of stars
Of matter between you and me thick as unattended webs
Time uncapsized but sail across
Workers in the morning shattering
Bottles against the cobblestones

It was like each quantum moment slowly
Exploding and reconstituting
These stones at the bottom of my glass
The gas that wants to combust
The liquid I drank passing through me

It's in my body a demand to be heard
To be seen
The day is lovely
It is winding around
My Berlin time coming to an end

Carry me back to the French shore to where my friend Eleanna
Took me in a kayak out onto the sea
For the man I thought I was going to be when I came here
For the changed and damaged one who is making his way home
He don't know which is true and which a lie
He wants to look back behind him at what's dead

*

B	R	I	G
H	T	B	Y
T	H	E	B
E	D	S	I
D	E	O	F

```
L     A     S     T

L     I     N     G

E     R     I     N

G     S     O     M

E     O     N     E.
```

*

There's no place that's home
Mostly I want to be alone
To be touched and loved
To drink water
To stretch and sleep

My animals wait for
My animal heart inside
I single out this one stairwell to go into and cry
One friend has moved away
Another is dead

Another I don't know where in the world he is but it isn't Moldova
What puzzle pieces fit
Take me back to my orbit
We are planets swung far
And yet

The wind through the stairwell
This body grown
Not by hunger but by lack
If god is a dog then he is the kind who kindly takes my hand in his mouth
The kind of friendly beast who wants to lick me everywhere

Held up into the sky
Soft and wet I am
The world
Walking forward into the dark
Not permitted to ever turn around

*

S	T	A	R
S	I	N	T
H	E	S	K
Y	A	R	E
S	E	E	N
I	N	S	H
A	P	E	S
O	N	L	Y
B	E	C	A
U	S	E	O
F	T	H	E
P	O	S	I
T	I	O	N
O	F	T	H

E	V	I	E
W	E	R	I
N	T	I	M
E	A	N	D
S	P	A	C
E	.	T	O
G	E	T	H
E	R	I	N
V	A	S	T
N	E	S	S
W	E	C	L
A	I	M	O
U	R	C	L
A	M	O	R.

★

Nobody really tells what it was Orpheus sang
To make even the dead freeze and groan
I imagine him lying facedown in the dirt
His arms stretched overhead
Singing verses down into the earth

+

This time not to stone
but you
smell the
dirt green
stereo you address

Epistle from the
archive of
eternity
death record the
dirt

    You press
your face
into
what is worship
    not of sky

    But I deep
    devour you
    silent and
        breathe
    opposite long years

Where you lay
in the night transcribing
sex
elevated yet
facedown

Eat dirt
    know this muck
    know your life
    blades brush
    your eyes

Life and
soft you
are held
around you day-
light around

You live then
      live
finally leave
the why
to know

Whether death or doubt— devote
yourself
down
smell
      the earth

Be not afraid
of what can carry
you immerse
immense
you to know now

Both sides
of death
I untaught unfolds its
frustrating
gift

Looking back at
heaven that
never was a
string that
could whole
him

Hold him
hole him
whole dim
hymn there
sings

He is held
by strings
helled
these cords that
changed him

Clang him
bell does not
clamor
he does not
clamor

Die or shall he
change
weave himself
hang or
hinge

He comes back
to life in music
rests against
the bodies
of no

He has not seen
the scene
the seas
he will not
know

+

So how do you pass through the days
Across borders borne by sky
the body is it the same
I try yoga try to run but
I am adrift unanchored unknown unspoken

Sitting next to an architect on the plane drawing in his pad
I want to be drawn plotted like that against paper
While I sit quietly recite old prayers whenever we take off or land
If someone hears me muttering in Arabic will they report me
Will I be allowed to fly

Gateway is different than gate
One keeps you out one leads you in
I return to the scene of what crime
I don't know what I
See here but I look back

*

W	R	O	U
G	H	T	S
A	C	R	E
D	S	C	R
U	M	Y	O
U	S	O	U
G	H	T	S
A	C	R	U
M	S	V	A

U   L   T   T

O   S   E   E

K   O   R   V

A   U   L   T

T   H   E   C

U   L   T   U

R   E   D   R

A   C   K   E

T   A   N   D

I   N   T   A

N   D   E   M

F   A   L   T

E   R   A   T

T   H   E   F

A   U   L   T

.   T   I   M

E   S   C   U

L   T   R   A

N   G   E   O

F   S   K   Y

M   Y   V   A

U   L   T   E

D   F   A   L

L   E   N   F

A   U   L   T.

*

The city is already
Different this sunny
Café the long lovely
Bike trail I ran on
This morning the dark

Front of the apartment
How would have
I dared to live
Late summer mosquitoes
I go and see the first

Edition of Paradise
Lost rushed to print while Milton
Feared he would be executed
For conspiracy and regicide
No I did not today

Press my forehead down
On clay or into the earth
To divine water words or breath
Up the river now and the words I wrote in the dark
I can barely breathe

To discern the handwriting of the book I wrote
Lying facedown in the damp earth
I actually have to retrace
The scrawled words with my hand
Can't channel that through crystal

Molt my wings and be born
Once more god help me
Phosphorus the morning star
Was the brother of Hesperus
The evening star

Would be a thousand more years or more before they learned
The two stars are the same star and not even a star
But a planet
Dusk do keep me up all night
With dumb questions and pointless chatter

*

O	R	I	V
E	R	I	T
H	A	S	B
E	E	N	S
O	M	E	L
O	N	G	T
I	M	E	S
E	R	E	I
E	N	D	E

A   V   O   R

E   D   T   H

Y   T   O   N

G   U   E   .

*

What I must know I must
Were the actual syllables Orpheus sang
To the dead to be allowed into hell allowed again to leave
With what was dead following behind
And then by doubting his song made queer and torn to pieces and cast in the river

*

O   H   D   O

G   I   N   H

E   A   V   E

N   G   O   D

O   W   N   O

N   M   E   .

Wrong Star

Wrong star I chose
To sail under alone
I did not want
To be alone
Brought or abandoned
Those nights when
I did not know
Who could know
Am I invited
Do you remember
Which question
Needs answer

Notes

After initially lodging charges and suspending him from employment, Yale University declined to press suit against Corey Menafee and offered him his old position back. He returned to work as a dining room attendant and became active in the movement to rename Calhoun College, where his action took place. The college was eventually renamed for Grace Hopper, computer scientist, mathematician, and naval admiral. The window was given to the collections of the Yale Art Museum, where then conservator Carol Snow made the decision not to restore the window but rather exhibit it in its shattered state.

Mohammed El-Khatib was invited by Carl Lewis to come to Texas and train with him. Though he did not qualify for the 2016 Olympics, he is again training with Lewis for 2020.

Sheila Chandra, after many years, has regained some use of her speaking voice.

Acknowledgments

"Recite" and "Wrong Star" previously appeared in *Seneca Review*.

"Hesperine for David Berger" previously appeared on the Academy of American Poets website, www.poets.org, as part of a project commemorating the 50th anniversary of the US Parks Department.

"Know No Name," appeared on the Poetry Foundation website, www.poetry-foundation.org, as part of their audio series *Poetry Off the Shelf*.

"The Voice of Sheila Chandra" appeared in *The Georgia Review*; excerpts had previously appeared in *Poetry*.

"Tagaq Sutra" appeared in *bæst: a journal of queer forms and affects*.

"Phosphorus" appeared in *American Poetry Review*.

Gratitudes:

I am grateful to the BAU Institute and the Headlands Center for the Arts for fellowships that enabled the writing of these poems.

Eleanna Anagnos, CAConrad, Matthew Dickman, Rachel Jagoda, Vandana Khanna, Blas Falconer, Mary Fischer, Nat Marcus, and Marco Wilkinson accompanied me in the making. Thank you to Ryan Murphy and Allison Benis White for your compelling work that inspired me. For more than can be expressed, thank you Fanny Howe.

Contents

RECENT TITLES FROM ALICE JAMES BOOKS

Arrow, Sumita Chakraborty
Country, Living, Ira Sadoff
Hot with the Bad Things, Lucia LoTempio
Witch, Philip Matthews
Neck of the Woods, Amy Woolard
Little Envelope of Earth Conditions, Cori A. Winrock
Aviva-No, Shimon Adaf, Translated by Yael Segalovitz
Half/Life: New & Selected Poems, Jeffrey Thomson
Odes to Lithium, Shira Erlichman
Here All Night, Jill McDonough
To the Wren: Collected & New Poems, Jane Mead
Angel Bones, Ilyse Kusnetz
Monsters I Have Been, Kenji C. Liu
Soft Science, Franny Choi
Bicycle in a Ransacked City: An Elegy, Andrés Cerpa
Anaphora, Kevin Goodan
Ghost, like a Place, Iain Haley Pollock
Isako Isako, Mia Ayumi Malhotra
Of Marriage, Nicole Cooley
The English Boat, Donald Revell
We, the Almighty Fires, Anna Rose Welch
DiVida, Monica A. Hand
pray me stay eager, Ellen Doré Watson
Some Say the Lark, Jennifer Chang
Calling a Wolf a Wolf, Kaveh Akbar
We're On: A June Jordan Reader, Edited by Christoph Keller and Jan Heller Levi
Daylily Called It a Dangerous Moment, Alessandra Lynch
Surgical Wing, Kristin Robertson
The Blessing of Dark Water, Elizabeth Lyons
Reaper, Jill McDonough
Madwoman, Shara McCallum

Alice James Books is committed to publishing books that matter. The press was founded in 1973 in Boston, Massachusetts as a cooperative, wherein authors performed the day-to-day undertakings of the press. This element remains present today, as authors who publish with the press are invited to collaborate closely in the publication process of their work. AJB remains committed to its founders' original feminist mission, while expanding upon the scope to include all voices and poets who might otherwise go unheard. In keeping with its efforts to build equity and increase inclusivity in publishing and the literary arts, AJB seeks out poets whose writing possesses the range, depth, and ability to cultivate empathy in our world and to dynamically push against silence. The press was named for Alice James, sister to William and Henry, whose extraordinary gift for writing went unrecognized during her lifetime.

Designed by Alban Fischer
Printed by McNaughton & Gunn